W9-ALL-789

Published by Bob Adams, Inc.
260 Center Street, Holbrook, MA 02343

ISBN: 1-55850-102-9

Printed in the United States of America

A   B   C   D   E   F   G   H   I   J

COVER PHOTO: Maria Taglienti, The Image Bank

ILLUSTRATIONS: Shannon Hall

THE Baby Shower Book

Etiquette • Decorations • Games • Food

Pauline Glendenning

BOB ADAMS, INC.
PUBLISHERS
Holbrook, Massachusetts

Table of Contents

Chapter Seven
Opening Gifts

Chapter Eight

Preface

A baby shower is a party given by friends and relatives for expectant or new parents. Its purpose is to celebrate the joyous event by "showering" the parents with gifts and warm wishes for the new baby. This custom has been going on for years, primarily to help new parents with the costs of preparing for a baby, but also to give friends and relatives a chance to share in the joy and excitement of a new little one.

The Baby Shower Book is a complete and practical guide for new and experienced baby shower hostesses alike. It's filled with easy ideas on planning, suggestions for decorations, dozens of baby shower games, and lots of simple and tasty recipes.

New baby shower hostesses will probably find something helpful on almost every page—but experienced hostesses will discover plenty of unusual, creative tips and time-saving suggestions to help make their next shower a bigger success.

There are no strict rules governing baby showers. Feel free to organize your shower any way you choose, so long as that way is fun and provides a festive atmosphere for welcoming the new baby.

Happy showering!

Chapter One

Invitations

Invitations for a baby shower can be store-bought or homemade. Either way they should contain the following information:

- ❤ the name(s) of the parent(s) being honored
- ❤ the shower date, time, and location
- ❤ who is giving the shower
- ❤ how to R.S.V.P.

The next two pages contain samples of homemade invitations. The first can be made out of colored paper or cloth, then folded in the shape of a diaper and fastened with a small gold safety pin. The second can be done on paper and folded to resemble a bottle. Ribbon, lace, or stenciled patterns can be added to both for decoration.

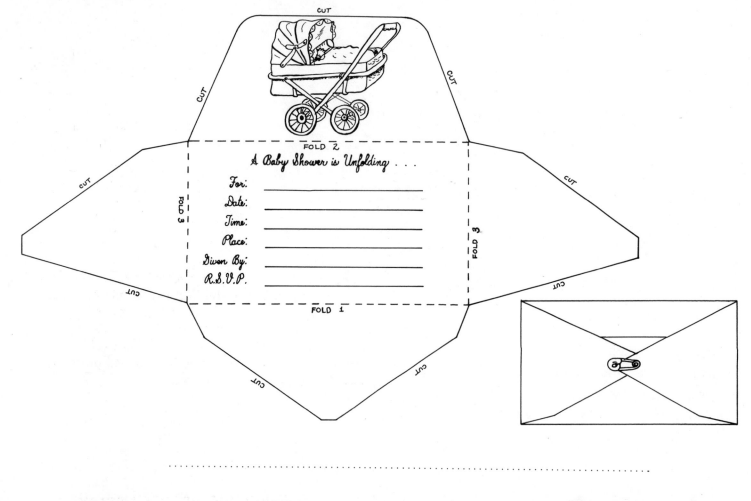

CUT

CUT

CUT

CUT

FOLD 2

A Baby Shower is Unfolding . . .

For: _____
Date: _____
Time: _____
Place: _____
Given By: _____
R.S.V.P. _____

FOLD 3

FOLD 3

FOLD 1

CUT

CUT

CUT

CUT

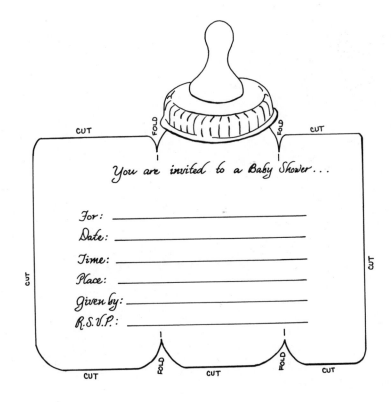

CUT · FOLD · FOLD · CUT

You are invited to a Baby Shower . . .

For: _____

Date: _____

Time: _____

Place: _____

Given by: _____

R.S.V.P.: _____

CUT · FOLD · CUT · FOLD · CUT

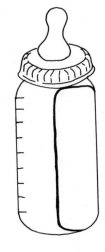

Chapter Two

Planning

FOR WHOM IS A SHOWER GIVEN?
Baby showers are most often given for the mother of a first child. A new trend is to give a shower for both the mother and father of a baby and invite other couples.

A shower can also be given for a couple having an unexpected or "caboose" baby, years after their other children were born. When this occurs, the parents have usually given away their baby items and need to start all over again.

It's perfectly acceptable to give a baby shower for new adoptive parents. Just like natural parents, they need baby necessities and would welcome warm wishes for their new child. However, the Mother of Honor (the person the shower is for) should be sure to let the guests know what size clothing the child needs, since adopted babies aren't always newborn.

THE SHOWER DATE—WHEN TO GIVE A SHOWER

In times past a baby shower was always given

before the baby was born, usually four to six weeks prior to the due date. The main advantage of this practice is that the expectant parents will receive much of what they need and so be more prepared for the arrival of the baby.

Today, however, new parents are often given baby showers *after* their baby is born. Here the benefit is that the gender of the child is known, so guests can buy appropriate clothing gifts. In addition, the mother can bring the new baby to the shower for all the guests to see.

Consult the Mother of Honor for the best date. Once a date is chosen and invitations are sent out, keep in mind that babies have their own clocks and often arrive early or late. Be prepared to reschedule the shower if necessary.

THE SHOWER TIME

The time of day chosen for the shower will depend on the day and location selected. If it's a weekday, then the shower should be held in the evening to accommodate those who work, unless the party is planned by the mother's coworkers. If it's a Saturday or Sunday, the shower should be held in the afternoon or evening to let people sleep in, run weekend errands, or attend religious services.

THE SHOWER LOCATION

A baby shower can really be held anywhere. A home is the logical choice; however, to make a shower more interesting other locations may be used. If the guests are coworkers of the mother, the shower could be held at the office or in a restaurant. A group of relatives or friends could meet at a park or picnic pavilion. If you live in an apartment complex, the party room will work nicely. Whatever the location, it should provide adequate parking and be comfortable for all guests. Bear in mind that availability of some locations, such as office meeting rooms or apartment party rooms, may be limited.

THE SHOWER HOSTESS(ES)

Because a baby shower can involve a lot of work and expense, it's much easier if there's more than one hostess.

Anyone can host a baby shower. It was once improper etiquette for an immediate relative to give a baby shower. This is no longer the case. Whoever wishes to give a baby shower can do so, whether friend, relative, coworker, or acquaintance.

R.S.V.P.

R.S.V.P. is the abbreviation for the French phrase *répondez s'il vous plaît*, meaning "answer, if it pleasesyou." In other words, "let us know whether you will be coming to the party."

Unfortunately, even when R.S.V.P. information is included in an invitation, some people forget to respond. You'll often have to follow up on your own by calling the invited guests you haven't heard from. It's better to do this than to plan for a small number of people and have more guests show up than expected.

When guests R.S.V.P., they often ask what the Mother of Honor needs for the new baby. Some of the larger department stores have registries for baby gifts. It is up to the Mother of Honor to decide whether she wants to use this service (see pages 18 and 19). If she does, you can tell the guests which store she is registered at. Otherwise, to avoid duplication of gifts, ask the Mother of Honor exactly what she needs. You can then convey the needed items to the guests as they R.S.V.P. Some common necessities are receiving blankets, baby towels and wash cloths, diapers, diaper bag, T-shirts, sleepers, bibs, and bottles. If there is a larger, more expensive item that the mother needs, such as a stroller or a car seat, you may suggest that two or three guests go in on the gift together. Some more unusual gifts include film, a picture frame, a savings bond, or I.O.U.s for baby sitting or house cleaning.

THE GUEST LIST

About six weeks before the shower, ask the Mother of Honor for a complete list of all the people she would like you to invite, along with their addresses. Never assume that certain people *must* be invited. Some or all of these people may be on the guest list for another baby shower. For example, the Mother of Honor may be given showers by both relatives and coworkers, and she may want some of her friends to attend one shower and some to attend the other. For this reason it is best to follow the list of invitees to the letter.

Baby Gift Registry

Registry #: 165433
Page: 1

Printed: 05-13-92

Parents: Anne MacLeod and Joseph MacLeod
1234 May Street
Anytown, MN 55234

Baby Arrival: 07-03-92

To avoid duplication of gifts, please leave this form with a salesperson when you have finished shoppping.

ESSENTIAL CLOTHING
Wants/Has

Wants	Has	
4	1	Booties
6	2	Side Snap T-shirts
4	1	Onesie T-shirts
6	0	Sleepers (6-9 mo.)
4	0	Layette Gowns

YEAR-ROUND CLOTHING
Wants/Has

Wants	Has	
3	1	Jumpsuits
3	2	Sweat Suits
3	0	Overalls
3	0	Tops
1	0	Sweater

SPRING/SUMMER CLOTHING
Wants/Has

Wants	Has	
3	1	Sunsuits
4	0	Shorts/Tops
1	0	Swimsuits
1	0	Swim Coverup
1	1	Bonnet

FALL/WINTER CLOTHING
Wants/Has

Wants	Has	
2	0	Warm Hats
1	0	Mittens
1	0	Mitten Clips
1	0	Bunting Bag
1	0	Snow Suit

☆ ★ ☆ *Deluxe Department Store* ☆ ★ ☆

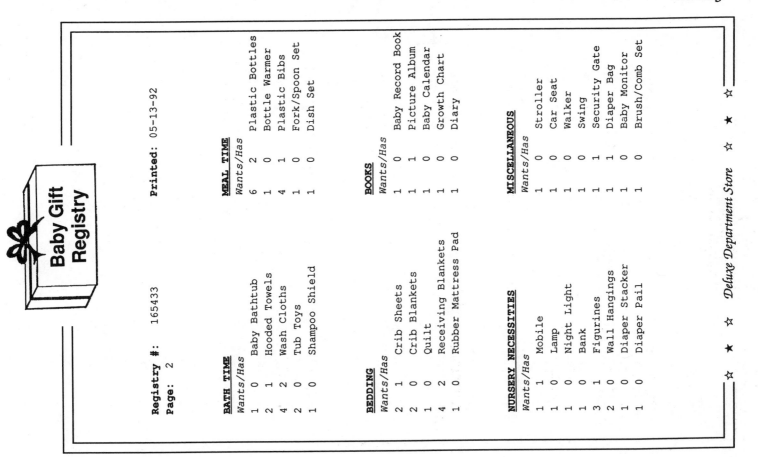

Baby Gift Registry

Registry #:   165433

Page: 2

Printed: 05-13-92

BATH TIME
Wants/Has

Wants	Has	Item
1	0	Baby Bathtub
2	1	Hooded Towels
4	2	Wash Cloths
2	0	Tub Toys
1	0	Shampoo Shield

BEDDING
Wants/Has

Wants	Has	Item
2	1	Crib Sheets
2	0	Crib Blankets
1	0	Quilt
4	2	Receiving Blankets
1	0	Rubber Mattress Pad

NURSERY NECESSITIES
Wants/Has

Wants	Has	Item
1	1	Mobile
1	0	Lamp
1	0	Night Light
1	0	Bank
3	1	Figurines
2	0	Wall Hangings
1	0	Diaper Stacker
1	0	Diaper Pail

MEAL TIME
Wants/Has

Wants	Has	Item
6	2	Plastic Bottles
1	0	Bottle Warmer
4	1	Plastic Bibs
1	0	Fork/Spoon Set
1	0	Dish Set

BOOKS
Wants/Has

Wants	Has	Item
1	0	Baby Record Book
1	1	Picture Album
1	0	Baby Calendar
1	0	Growth Chart
1	0	Diary

MISCELLANEOUS
Wants/Has

Wants	Has	Item
1	0	Stroller
1	0	Car Seat
1	0	Walker
1	0	Swing
1	1	Security Gate
1	1	Diaper Bag
1	0	Baby Monitor
1	0	Brush/Comb Set

☆ ★ ☆ ☆ *Deluxe Department Store* ☆ ★ ☆

Chapter Three

Decorations

Decorations are important for a baby shower because they make the party more festive and fun. Like anything else, decorations can be simple or elaborate, traditional or unique. It's your choice as to how many and what type of decorations are used. Paper product stores carry the basic balloons and streamers, but you'd be surprised at how many other items can be used as decorations. For example, toy wooden alphabet blocks can be scattered anywhere for a festive appearance.

Five or six new infant bibs can be placed in a circle around a punch bowl to look like flower petals. Use real baby's breath flowers and greens to decorate around a centerpiece. Baby bottles can be filled with candy to add color to a dessert table. Listed below are additional ideas for decorating themes.

BABY THEMES

Teddy Bears

Tie a bunch of balloons around a big teddy bear and set it in a chair. Borrow additional teddies from friends, put diapers on them, and position them around the shower location. Buy paper plates and napkins with teddy bears on them. Buy or make teddy bear-shaped cookies. Serve bear-shaped candies along with desserts.

Umbrellas

Hang a real umbrella from the ceiling, above the chair where the Mother of Honor will sit so she'll be "showered" in style. Smaller paper umbrellas or parasols can be purchased from paper product stores to use as table centerpieces. Purchase or make invitations with umbrellas. Garnish beverages with miniature paper umbrellas.

Cartoon or Television Characters

All kinds of items decorated with characters from Disney Babies, Muppet Babies, and Sesame Street are available in stores, including invitations, paper plates, napkins, and decorations. In fact, if the Mother of Honor particularly likes a certain set of characters, the hostess may want to suggest to guests that they purchase shower gifts decorated with the characters—crib sheets, blankets, T-shirts, plate sets, etc.

Trains

A buffet table can be decorated with a toy train; make your own by connecting boxes of animal crackers together with yarn. If it is known that the baby is a boy, a child's conductor cap could be a theme-related gift for the baby.

Baby Animals

Baby animals such as lambs, ducklings, kittens, and puppies can also be used as themes. Stuffed baby animals can be borrowed or purchased and placed around the shower location to set a scene. Play the "Baby Animals" game (see page 66). Make cut-out sugar cookies in the shape of baby animals (see page 115).

Miscellaneous

Other ideas for baby shower themes include storks, clowns, dolls, etc. Come up with your own!

HOLIDAY THEMES

Another way for a hostess to decorate the shower location is to use a holiday theme. Of course it will depend on what time of year the shower is being held and which holiday is closest. As you will discover, baby shower decorations aren't limited to just pink and blue.

New Year

Sprinkle confetti or glitter around the food table or punch bowl. Lots of multi-colored balloons, party horns, and even non-alcoholic champagne can be used to celebrate the new year and the new baby!

Valentine's Day

Decorate with red, pink, and white balloons, cardboard red hearts, and baby cupids (all available at paper product stores) taped up on walls or windows. Serve heart-shaped sugar cookies with red sugar sprinkles (see page 115) and red punch. Sprinkle Hershey's kisses around the dessert table for decoration.

St. Patrick's Day

Use dark green, light green, and white balloons and streamers. For dessert, serve shamrock-shaped sugar cookies with green sugar sprinkles, or a peppermint bon bon ice cream. Offer mint flavored coffee topped with whipped cream for a beverage. Small shamrock plants can be used for centerpieces and later given to the guests as they leave. Use Irish lace for decorating the food or gift table.

Easter

Decorate with pastel-colored balloons—pink, yellow, green, purple, and blue. Plastic Easter eggs can be filled with candy and used to decorate a food table, then later given to guests as party gifts. Use an Easter basket filled with plastic grass and decorated hard-boiled eggs for a centerpiece. Small stuffed bunnies can also be used to decorate a shower location.

Independence Day

Decorate with red, white, and blue balloons and streamers. Small flags can be scattered around the shower location. Play upbeat patriotic music in the background. For dessert, prepare a white cake, top with whipped cream, and decorate with fresh blueberries and strawberries in the design of a flag. Bring the cake out to the guests with a lighted sparkler on top. Remove the sparkler after it goes out; cut and serve pieces of cake with miniature 1" toothpick flags on top (available at baking supply stores).

Halloween

Decorate with orange, black, and white balloons. Miniature orange gourds that look like "baby" pumpkins can be used as centerpieces and later given to guests as party gifts. "Baby" ghosts can be made out of white tissues and strung together with black yarn to make unique streamers. Spread out spun cotton on a table with "baby" plastic spiders for a centerpiece. Prepare "Orange Sherbert Punch" (see page 117) for a beverage. If the shower is held after the baby is born, the new baby can come to the shower dressed in a pumpkin costume.

Christmas

Use red, green, and white balloons and streamers. A miniature decorated Christmas tree, little angels, or stars can be used for centerpieces. Serve egg nog or hot apple cider with cinnamon sticks for beverages. Use holly to decorate around a punch bowl or food table. Play Christmas carols in the background to set the mood. You're celebrating not only the birth of Christ but the birth of another baby!

CORSAGE

Getting a corsage for the Mother of Honor is a nice touch, one that makes her feel special. A corsage made with real flowers can be ordered from a florist, but a homemade one is easy to make and more practical.

Materials Needed

1 Teething ring or rattle (one with two holes works best—rocking horse, pretzel)

¼ Yard tulle fabric (netting)

1 Package small silk flowers with wire stems

1 Foot of 1" eyelet trim

1 Large safety pin

Instructions (see illustration next page)

1. Gather fabric along the width, bringing the short ends together.

2. Hold gathered fabric in center and fold in half. Pull folded center of fabric through one hole and back out the other hole of the teething ring, just far enough to stay in place by itself. Fan or spread out top outer edges of fabric evenly.

3. Poke wire stems of silk flowers through fabric (in the front and out the back) and twist wire ends to knot in back.

4. From the back, encircle whole corsage with eyelet trim and tuck ends behind teething ring. Cut excess trim.

5. Pin corsage onto Mother of Honor with a large safety pin.

Note: Don't glue any materials to the teething ring. The object is to be able to disassemble the corsage easily after the shower so the baby can use the teething ring or rattle. If needed, extra safety pins can be used (from behind) to keep the netting and trim in place.

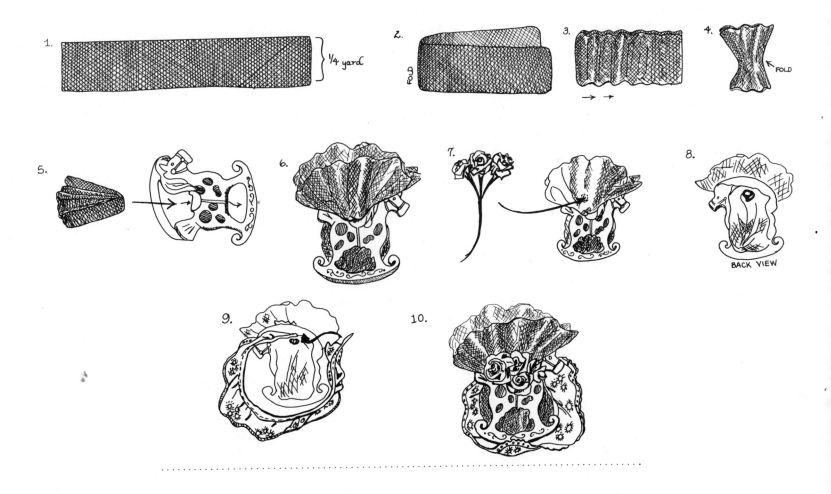

1.

¼ yard

2.

FOLD

3.

4.

FOLD

5.

6.

7.

8.

BACK VIEW

9.

10.

Chapter Four

Starting the Shower

- The Mother of Honor should arrive at the shower location a few minutes early in order to be present when the guests arrive.
- Pin the corsage on the Mother of Honor.
- Seat the Mother of Honor in a comfortable chair in the corner of the room. Seating works best if chairs for guests are arranged in a circle facing the Mother of Honor.
- Greet all shower guests as they arrive and introduce them to each other.
- Shower gifts should be set aside in one location for opening later.
- Once the guests are seated, offer them a beverage.
- Assign someone to take a few pictures during the shower for the baby's scrapbook.

Chapter Five

Games

After everyone is introduced, the first function of the shower should be to play at least one game so that guests can mingle and get to know each other. Prizes for games don't have to be extravagant. Small, inexpensive, useful items work well: note paper, hot pads or oven mitts, potpourri, refrigerator magnets, candy, etc.

BABY CROSSWORD PUZZLE
(see next two pages)

Needed: Photocopies of "Baby Crossword Puzzle" game sheets; pencils with erasers; magazines to write on.

Objective: The players try to fill in as many correct answers as they can in five minutes.

The player with the most correct answers wins.

. . . .

Baby Crossword Puzzle

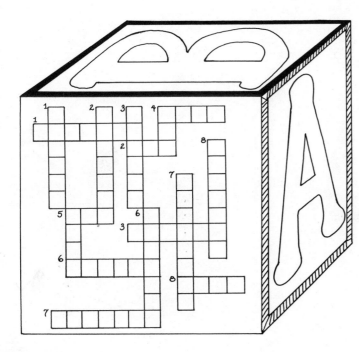

DOWN

1. Moving chair used to put baby to sleep.

2. Song for baby.

3. Baby's toy that makes noise when shaken.

4. Keeps baby's clothes clean while baby eats.

5. Where baby sleeps.

6. Baby's socks.

7. Sooths baby's teething gums.

8. Covers baby to keep warm.

ACROSS

1. Baby's drink.

2. Where baby gets bath.

3. Attaches to crib, moves around to entertain baby.

4. Released air bubble.

5. What baby does when un-happy.

6. Baby's hat.

7. Keep baby's bottom dry.

8. These are blue for most babies when they're born.

Baby Crossword Puzzle

(correct answers)

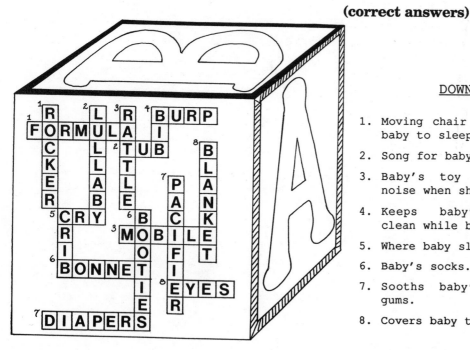

DOWN

1. Moving chair used to put baby to sleep.

2. Song for baby.

3. Baby's toy that makes noise when shaken.

4. Keeps baby's clothes clean while baby eats.

5. Where baby sleeps.

6. Baby's socks.

7. Sooths baby's teething gums.

8. Covers baby to keep warm.

ACROSS

1. Baby's drink.

2. Where baby gets bath.

3. Attaches to crib, moves around to entertain baby.

4. Released air bubble.

5. What baby does when unhappy.

6. Baby's hat.

7. Keep baby's bottom dry.

8. These are blue for most babies when they're born.

BOTTLED DICE

Needed: Two dice; one baby bottle; one plastic baby wipe container (empty) with the top off; wrapped prizes placed in the center of the room.

Objective: The game is timed for ten minutes. As everyone sits in a circle, players take turns shaking the dice in the bottle and throwing them into the container. Whoever throws doubles gets to take a prize from the center of the room. When all the prizes are gone, winners can take prizes from other winners.

When the time is up, whoever has a prize gets to keep it.

MYSTERY BABY CUISINE
(see illustrations on pages 38, 39, and 40)

Needed: Fifteen jars of baby food (all different—no blends); masking tape; pencils; magazines to write on.

Prior to game: Take the labels off the jars of baby food one at a time. Be careful to document what is in each of the jars, as you put a piece of masking tape with an assigned number on each jar.

Take a piece of paper and number it one to fifteen. List along the side the possible baby food choices (mixed up). Make enough photocopies for all of the players.

Put all of the numbered jars of baby food on a TV tray in the middle of the room.

Pass out a magazine, a copy of the game sheet, and a pencil to each of the players.

Objective: To guess what kind of baby food is in each of the numbered jars.

Players can pick up and examine the jars. It takes about ten to fifteen minutes to guess.

The person with the most correct answers wins.

Note: This isn't easy, since pears look like applesauce, squash looks like carrots or sweet potatoes, etc. When the game is finished, the hostess should tape the correct labels to each of the baby food jars and give them to the Mother of Honor for her baby.

Mystery Baby Cuisine

1._____

2._____

3._____

4._____

5._____

6._____

7._____

8._____

9._____

10._____

11._____

12._____

13._____

14._____

15._____

Green Beans	Beets
Prunes	Apricots
Squash	Peas
Sweet Potatoes	Blueberries
Bananas	Applesauce
Pears	Plums
Peaches	Corn
Carrots	

Mystery Baby Cuisine
(correct answers)

1. Pears

2. Apricots

3. Blueberries

4. Peas

5. Corn

6. Plums

7. Sweet Potatoes

8. Applesauce

9. Prunes

10. Peaches

11. Carrots

12. Green Beans

13. Squash

14. Bananas

15. Beets

BABY ALL GROWN UP

(see illustrations on next three pages)

Needed: Six brown lunch bags; a marker; paper; scissors.

Prior to game: Write the following categories with marker on lunch bags: GENDER, PHYSICAL TRAITS, HOBBIES, TALENTS, OCCUPATION, and MISC. Then make up possibilities for each category, write them on slips of paper, and deposit them in their appropriate bag. Note: eliminate the gender category if the sex of the baby is known.

Objective: Players will try to predict what the baby will be like "all grown up." Players are divided into teams of two. Each team gets to take one slip of paper out of each bag, except for the MISC. bag (take two). When all of the teams have all of their slips, each team describes their "grown up baby" to the Mother of Honor. A possible "grown up baby" may be: a boy who has baby blue eyes and long lashes, is a professional baseball player who lives in Hawaii, does Yoga every morning, has perfect handwriting, and drives a Mercedes.

Winner: The Mother of Honor chooses which person she would like her baby to be. Each member of the winning team gets a prize.

GENDER	Girl	Boy	Girl	Boy	Girl
PHYSICAL TRAITS	Has curly red hair and freckles.	Has thick brown hair and bushy eyebrows.	Has straight black hair and dimples.	Has wavy brown hair and straight white teeth.	Has baby blue eyes and long lashes.
HOBBIES	Collects stamps.	Does Yoga every morning.	Goes to the opera twice a month.	Likes to bake chocolate chip cookies.	Grows rare African violets.
TALENTS	Is a great story and joke teller.	Can sing the Star Spangled Banner on key.	Knows how to juggle.	Is an excellent horseback rider.	Can hold his/her breath underwater for four minutes.
OCCUPATION	Is a private investigator.	Is a gourmet chef in France.	Is a professional baseball player.	Owns an apple orchard.	Is a bee keeper.
MISC.	Has a moped.	Has a French poodle named Fifi.	Makes his/her bed *every* morning.	Lives in Hawaii.	Likes peanut butter and jelly sandwiches.

Boy	Girl	Boy	Girl	Boy	Girl
Is very tall, dark, and handsome.	Has dark brown eyes and wears wire rimmed glasses.	Has short blond hair and small ears.	Has hazel eyes and sandy blond hair.	Has emerald green eyes and a friendly smile.	Has a perfect nose.
Likes to parachute jump from airplanes.	Is hooked on soap operas.	Grows herbs for the local Farmers' Market.	Likes to play Solitaire—and never cheats.	Makes homemade strawberry jam.	Plays a mean game of poker.
Has a green thumb with houseplants.	Is great with kids.	Knows seven languages including Pig Latin.	Has perfect handwriting.	Is a speed reader.	Has an I.Q. of 368.
Is an over-the-road truck driver.	Is an eighth grade math teacher.	Breeds thoroughbred Arabian horses.	Is a fortune teller in the circus.	Is a Hollywood movie star.	Is an aerobics instructor.
Believes in U.F.O.'s.	Drives a Mercedes.	Always moves the furniture when he/she vacuums.	Likes his/her eggs easy over.	Is a member of the PTA—has five kids.	Has a solar powered house.

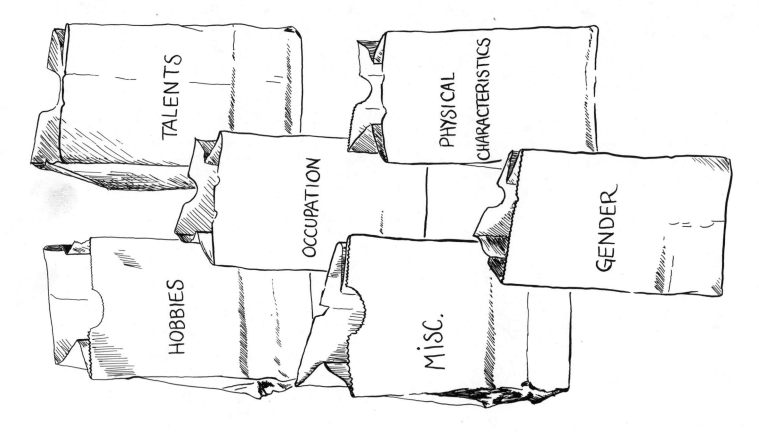

SEARCH FOR BABY PINS

Needed: One pie pan; uncooked white rice; one package of small gold "baby" safety pins; a blindfold; a stopwatch or watch with a second hand.

Objective: To find, blindfolded, the baby pins in a pan of rice. Each player is timed for two minutes.

The person who finds the most pins wins.

Note: This is not easy to do while blindfolded, because the rice and pins feel similar and slip through your fingers.

TUMBLED BABY WORDS
(see next two pages)

Needed: Photocopies of "Tumbled Baby Words" game sheets on blue and/or pink paper if possible; pencils; magazines to write on; a stopwatch or watch with a second hand.

Prior to game: Take fifteen words associated with babies and mix up (tumble) their letters. Then make enough copies for each guest.

Objective: Players are timed for five minutes while they try to unscramble the fifteen baby words.

The person who has the most correct answers wins.

Tumbled Baby Words

1. teblot   _____

2. cirifepa   _____

3. predia   _____

4. sentabis   _____

5. kletnab   _____

6. tralte   _____

7. larkew   _____

8. yelppna   _____

9. bric   _____

10. crekor   _____

11. nobten   _____

12. soibtoe   _____

13. roltserl   _____

14. murfola   _____

15. werdop   _____

Tumbled Baby Words
(correct answers)

1. bottle

2. pacifier

3. diaper

4. bassinet

5. blanket

6. rattle

7. walker

8. playpen

9. crib

10. rocker

11. bonnet

12. booties

13. stroller

14. formula

15. powder

DIAPER BABY

Needed: One large baby doll; one cloth diaper; two diaper pins; one pair of mittens; a stopwatch or watch with a second hand.

Objective: Players take turns diapering the baby doll while wearing mittens.

The person who gets the fastest time wins.

BOTTLED CANDY

Needed: One new baby bottle and enough candy to fill the bottle (gummy bears or peas and carrots candy).

Prior to game: Count the pieces of candy before putting them into the bottle.

Objective: Each player guesses how many pieces of candy are in the baby bottle.

Whoever guesses closest to the actual number wins.

Note: When the game is over, the baby bottle is given to the Mother of Honor for her new baby to use.

HIDDEN BABY NAMES

(see next two pages)

Needed: Photocopies of "Hidden Baby Names" game sheets on blue and/or pink paper if possible; pencils; magazines to write on.

Prior to game: Create a game sheet by placing baby names on a piece of graph paper going all directions—forward, backward, up, down, and diagonally. Fill in the other squares with miscellaneous letters. Make sure to list the possible names along the right side to help the players in their search.

Objective: To find the hidden baby names provided on the side of the game sheet..Players are timed for five minutes.

The person who finds the most names wins.

```
A  X  C  D  E  M  L  R  J  A  M  E  S  N  J  A  V  S
Y  E  I  L  E  E  N  U  F  R  I  M  I  A  K  T  U  O
R  Z  N  T  V  X  I  J  A  Z  E  B  O  Z  A  S  I  L
A  O  K  A  F  A  C  N  Z  P  O  K  Y  G  A  I  S  A
H  S  H  N  J  O  H  B  A  R  A  S  U  N  O  D  G  N
C  Y  S  O  B  I  O  T  X  M  C  B  T  C  E  O  X  I
A  R  O  A  J  Y  L  S  A  M  O  H  T  T  B  M  I  T
Z  V  J  O  H  N  A  P  O  N  I  D  I  B  H  X  A  S
W  L  K  Z  X  A  S  R  T  D  I  W  M  E  L  K  G  U
R  O  B  E  R  T  K  V  Q  R  Y  G  O  Z  I  A  H  J
E  J  D  M  X  H  Z  O  L  F  U  B  T  Q  R  R  I  K
L  S  I  U  M  B  Y  R  A  M  M  Y  N  Y  Y  G  Z  R
L  N  O  T  D  L  W  E  C  K  E  A  A  D  N  A  M  A
I  F  A  R  G  P  N  F  A  T  R  I  A  B  A  R  X  T
N  E  Z  K  X  A  M  I  C  H  A  E  L  K  T  W  Y  J
D  G  N  A  I  T  C  N  V  E  A  N  N  A  T  S  G  E
S  C  S  R  Z  K  D  N  S  N  J  H  N  Q  I  V  A  S
E  F  B  X  Y  Z  E  E  U  R  W  I  G  Y  R  P  Z  S
Y  P  A  R  B  C  P  J  G  Y  T  E  Z  E  B  X  S  I
S  N  E  R  A  K  J  H  E  A  M  N  I  Z  U  K  A  C
Y  E  S  R  T  N  P  Y  C  P  G  K  Y  T  V  T  U  A
E  R  H  V  Z  E  D  O  U  G  L  A  S  Y  A  E  X  T
I  U  G  P  S  M  X  O  G  O  X  S  V  M  U  K  O  C
U  A  T  O  E  L  E  I  N  A  D  R  M  W  I  A  F  G
J  L  J  R  W  S  I  Q  K  Q  J  Y  A  A  H  J  O  G
```

Amanda	James	Michael
Anita	Jane	Nicholas
Anna	Jennifer	Paul
Blair	Jessica	Robert
Brandon	John	Robin
Brian	Joseph	Rose
Brittany	Josh	Sara
Daniel	Justin	Susan
Douglas	Karen	Tammy
Eileen	Katie	Ted
Gary	Lauren	Thomas
Gina	Lindsey	Zachary
Henry	Lisa	
Jake	Mary	

Amanda
Anita
Anna
Blair
Brandon
Brian
Brittany
Daniel
Douglas
Eileen
Gary
Gina
Henry
Jake

James
Jane
Jennifer
Jessica
John
Joseph
Josh
Justin
Karen
Katie
Lauren
Lindsey
Lisa
Mary

Michael
Nicholas
Paul
Robert
Robin
Rose
Sara
Susan
Tammy
Ted
Thomas
Zachary

THE CLOTHESPIN GAME

Needed: One clip-type clothespin for each player.

Objective: At the beginning of the shower, a clothespin is clipped to the collar or lapel of each guest. If someone hears another guest saying the word "baby" at any time throughout the shower, they get to take that person's clothespin and put it on.

The person with the most clothespins at the end of the shower wins.

This game can keep a shower lively. People don't realize how hard it is to not say the word "baby" at a baby shower. Another variation of this game is to have players take clothespins when other players say the word "I" instead of "baby."

NAMING BABY

Needed: Paper; pencils; magazines to write on.

Objective: Give each player a blank piece of paper, a pencil, and a magazine. Announce a category of names (see next page) such as names ending in "en," "er," "y," "ie," "ine," or "a," and tell the players to write down as many names as they can think of. Each category is timed for two minutes.

The person with the most names wins. A prize can be given for each category or all categories together.

. . . .

Naming Baby

"en" ending

Allen	Hellen
Arlen	Karen
Carmen	Lauren
Ellen	Steven
Gretchen	Warren

"er" ending

Amber	Jennifer
Baxter	Peter
Carter	Roger
Esther	Walter
Heather	Webster

"ie" ending

Angie	Lennie
Bernie	Leslie
Bobbie	Marie
Bonnie	Marjorie
Connie	Melanie
Jeannie	Millie
Joanie	Reggie
Julie	Stephanie
Katie	Susie
Laurie	Valerie

"y" ending

Amy	Jeffrey	Peggy
Becky	Jerry	Perry
Billy	Jimmy	Polly
Bobby	Johnny	Ricky
Bradley	Judy	Sally
Brittany	Kathy	Sandy
Danny	Kimberly	Tammy
Darcy	Larry	Terry
Emily	Mary	Timothy
Gary	Melody	Tony
Gregory	Molly	Tracy
Holly	Nancy	Trudy

"ine/een/ene" ending

Adeline	Jeanine
Christine	Joleen
Colleen	Josephine
Corrine	Karleen
Darlene	Kathleen
Earleen	Marleen
Eileen	Maureen
Francine	Nadine
Geraldine	Norine
Jacqueline	Pauline

"a" ending

Amanda	Donna	Laura	Paula	Sara
Anna	Emma	Lea	Rebecca	Sheila
Barbara	Georgia	Linda	Rhoda	Tanya
Briana	Gina	Lisa	Rita	Teresa
Cecilia	Gloria	Monica	Roberta	Tina
Cynthia	Greta	Pamela	Rosa	Virginia
Debra	Jenna	Patricia	Sandra	Wanda

Note: **This is just a sampling of the answers.**

BABY BINGO

Needed: Photocopies of the "Baby Bingo" game sheets (see next page); pencils; magazines to write on.

Prior to game: Make a game sheet by listing six three-letter, six four-letter, six five-letter, six six-letter, and six seven-letter baby words under a bingo box with a few free spaces. Then write each possible word on a piece of paper and put them all in a basket.

Objective: Before the game starts the players fill in the blank squares on the board with one word from each category, putting letters in horizontally from left to right. For example, they would choose one three-letter word and write it in the second row, choose one four-letter word and write it in the third row, etc. until all squares are filled in (see sample). Each player's card should be different. When everyone is ready, draw words from the basket, one by one, calling them out each time. When a player has a word on her card, she circles it.

The player who is first to get all her words circled says "BINGO" and wins. *Note:* after the first winner wins, the game can continue until there's a second and/or third winner.

	B	A	B	Y	*	*	*
Row #1	B	A	B	Y	*	*	*
Row #2	I	*	*	*				(3)
Row #3	N	*	*					(4)
Row #4	G	*						(5)
Row #5	O							(6)
Row #6								(7)

→

(INSERT WORD CHOICES FROM LEFT TO RIGHT)

LETTERS PER WORD

<u>Three</u>	<u>Four</u>	<u>Five</u>
bib	comb	spoon
cry	pins	sleep
wet	burp	drink
dry	crib	swing
toy	bath	juice
nuk	soft	colic

<u>Six</u>	<u>Seven</u>
rattle	formula
bottle	nursery
diaper	blanket
cradle	lullaby
bootie	playpen
bonnet	feeding

LETTERS PER WORD

Three	Four	Five
bib	comb	spoon
cry	pins	sleep
wet	burp	drink
dry	crib	swing
toy	bath	juice
nuk	soft	colic

Six	Seven
rattle	formula
bottle	nursery
diaper	blanket
cradle	lullaby
bootie	playpen
bonnet	feeding

B	**A**	**B**	**Y**	*	*	*
I	*	*	*	b	i	b
N	*	*	s	o	f	t
G	*	s	p	o	o	n
O	r	a	t	t	l	e
l	u	l	l	a	b	y

Row #1
Row #2 (3)
Row #3 (4)
Row #4 (5)
Row #5 (6)
Row #6 (7)

→

(INSERT WORD CHOICES FROM LEFT TO RIGHT)

NURSERY RHYME RIDDLES

(see next two pages)

Needed: Photocopies of "Nursery Rhyme Riddles" game sheets; pencils; magazines to write on.

Objective: To provide answers for the questions. The game is timed for five minutes.

The player with the most correct answers wins.

Nursery Rhyme Riddles

1. What did Peter Piper pick?

2. Who were the three men in a tub?

3. What did Georgie Porgie do to the girls to make them cry?

4. Who did the three blind mice run after?

5. What is Tuesday's child full of?

6. How many blackbirds were baked in a pie?

7. What did Little Miss Muffet sit on?

8. What was Little Jack Horner eating in the corner?

9. What did Mother Hubbard go to the cupboard for?

10. What did Tommy Tucker sing for?

11. Whom did Simple Simon meet going to the fair?

12. What kind of flowers grew in Mistress Mary's garden?

13. What did Tom the Piper's son steal?

14. What was Wee Willie Winkie wearing when he ran through town?

15. How much wool did the black sheep have?

16. Where did Doctor Foster go?

17. Where did the wise old owl live?

18. What was Yankee Doodle riding on when he went to town?

19. How old was the pease-porridge in the pot?

20. In Hickery, Dickery, Dock, what time did the mouse run down the clock?

21. What couldn't Jack Sprat eat?

22. What was the cat playing when the cow jumped over the moon?

23. What did the three little kittens lose?

24. What was Humpty Dumpty sitting on before he fell?

Nursery Rhyme Riddles
(correct answers)

1. A peck of pickled peppers
2. The butcher, baker, and candlestick maker
3. Kissed them
4. The farmer's wife
5. Grace
6. Four and twenty
7. A tuffet
8. A Christmas pie
9. A bone for her dog
10. His supper
11. A pieman
12. Silver bells
13. A pig
14. His nightgown

15. Three bags full
16. Gloucester
17. In an oak
18. A pony
19. Nine days old
20. One o'clock
21. Fat
22. A fiddle
23. Their mittens
24. A wall

DIMENSIONS

Needed: One full roll of toilet paper.

Objective: Take a roll of toilet paper and ask each player to tear off as long a section as she wants. However, do not tell the players how the squares will be used. Then ask the Mother of Honor to stand up. Have her hold one end of the roll of toilet paper while you roll it around her waist, measuring the circumference of mom and baby. The correct length of paper is then compared to each player's piece.

Winner: The person whose piece of toilet paper is closest to the correct circumference of mom and baby.

WHO'S THAT BABY?

Needed: Paper; pencils; magazines to write on; a bulletin board; stick pins; a baby picture of each guest.

Prior to shower: When guests R.S.V.P., ask them to bring a baby picture of themselves to the shower each with the guest's name written on the back.

Objective: Pin all of the guests' baby pictures up on a bulletin board and assign a number to each photo (see next page). Players number a sheet of paper according to the number of pictures. Everyone gets ten minutes to guess who each baby is and to write down the person's name by the appropriate number.

The player who guesses the most baby pictures correctly wins.

BABY ANIMALS
(see next two pages)

Needed: Photocopies of "Baby Animals" game sheets; pencils; magazines to write on.

Objective: Tell players to write down the term used to describe the baby of each animal. The game is timed for five minutes.

Winner: The player who has the most baby animal terms correct.

Baby Animals

What do you call a baby . . .

1. buffalo _____
2. cat _____
3. cow _____
4. deer _____
5. dog _____
6. eagle _____
7. elephant _____
8. frog _____
9. giraffe _____
10. goat _____
11. goose _____
12. grouse _____

13. hawk _____
14. horse _____
15. kangaroo _____
16. moose _____
17. pig _____
18. rabbit _____
19. raccoon _____
20. sheep _____
21. swan _____
22. turkey _____
23. whale _____
24. zebra _____

Baby Animals
(correct answers)

1. buffalo — calf
2. cat — kitten
3. cow — calf
4. deer — fawn
5. dog — puppy
6. eagle — eaglet
7. elephant — calf
8. frog — tadpole
9. giraffe — calf
10. goat — kid
11. goose — gosling
12. grouse — poult
13. hawk — chick
14. horse — colt, filly, foal
15. kangaroo — joey
16. moose — calf
17. pig — piglet
18. rabbit — bunny
19. raccoon — kit
20. sheep — lamb
21. swan — cygnet
22. turkey — poult
23. whale — calf
24. zebra — colt

SHOPPING FOR BABY

(see next two pages)

Needed: Photocopies of "Shopping for Baby" game sheets for each of the players; pencils; magazines to write on.

Objective: Players try to match each brand name on the left with an item on the right.

The first player to get all answers correct wins.

Shopping for Baby

When mom made the shopping list for baby, she wrote down only the brand names. You offered to do the shopping, but need help figuring out what each item is. Match each brand name on the left with an item on the right.

ZWIEBACK _____	formula	**Q-TIPS** _____	formula
NUM ZIT _____	bottle	**BABYLAX** _____	stain remover
LUVS _____	laundry detergent	**DREFT** _____	sun block lotion
DESITIN _____	acetaminophen	**JOHNSON'S** _____	baby wipes
SIMILAC _____	cotton swabs	**PANADOL** _____	diaper rash ointment
PEDIALYTE _____	teething toast	**ISOMIL** _____	pacifier
CHUBS _____	fabric softener	**SNUGGLE** _____	baby laxative
EVENFLOW _____	diapers		
HUGGIES _____	maintenance water		
WATER BABIES _____	teething pain medicine		
NUK _____	baby powder		
SHOUT _____	diapers		

Shopping for Baby
(correct answers)

ZWIEBACK — teething toast

NUM ZIT — teething pain medicine

LUVS — diapers

DESITIN — diaper rash ointment

SIMILAC — formula

PEDIALYTE — maintenance water

CHUBS — baby wipes

EVENFLOW — bottle

HUGGIES — diapers

WATER BABIES — sun block lotion

NUK — pacifier

SHOUT — stain remover

Q-TIPS — cotton swabs

BABYLAX — baby laxative

DREFT — laundry detergent

JOHNSON'S — baby powder

PANADOL — acetaminophen

ISOMIL — formula

SNUGGLE — fabric softener

BABY BLOCK BUILDERS

Needed: Enough alphabet baby blocks for each player to have one.

Objective: Give each player a baby block and divide players into teams of two or three (depending on the total number of guests). Each team must use all of the letters on their blocks to form words that start with their letters, and then put those words together to form a complete sentence about a baby. Additional words can be used in between the required letter words to enhance the sentences. Players should try to be creative and original (see next page for examples). Teams are given ten minutes. When every team has prepared its baby sentence, each team recites it to the Mother of Honor.

Winner: The Mother of Honor chooses the baby sentence that she likes the best. Every member of the winning team gets a prize.

Little Alice Rolled to the Edge of the Quilt
when she saw her Daddy.

Baby Sam Giggled
when the Kitty Jumped on the Xylophone.

NURSERY FIND

(see next two pages)

Needed: Photocopies of a drawing of a nursery with hidden objects; pencils; magazines to write on.

Objective: Players try to find and circle the hidden objects in the nursery drawing. Everyone is timed for ten minutes.

The player who finds the most objects wins.

Find and circle the objects hidden in the baby's nursery: baseball, crayon, horseshoe, diaper pin, spoon, story book, tea cup, Band-Aid, banana, baby bottle, comb, Q-tip, diamond ring, eye glasses, fork.

TELEVISION TOTS TRIVIA
(see next three pages)

Needed: Photocopies of "Television Tots Trivia" game sheets; pencils; magazines to write on.

Prior to shower: Make up a list of questions asking the character names of babies and children (tots) on television shows.

Objective: Players try to guess the correct character name(s) described in each television show. Everyone is timed for ten minutes.

The player with the most television character names correct wins.

Television Tots Trivia

1. On "I Love Lucy" what is the name of Lucy & Ricky Ricardo's son? _____

2. On "Little House on the Prairie" what are the names of Charles and Caroline Ingalls' three daughters? _____, _____ and _____

3. On "The Little Rascals" whose heart is Alfalfa always trying to win? _____ Who is the bully? _____

4. On "The Jetsons" what are the names of George and Jane's daughter? _____ and son? _____

5. On "The Addams Family" what are the names of Morticia and Gomez's daughter? _____ and son? _____

6. On "My Three Sons" what are the names of Robbie and Kathleeen Douglas's triplets? _____, _____ and _____

7. On "The Munsters" what is the name of Herman and Lily's son? _____

8. On "The Waltons" what is the name of John and Olivia's youngest daughter? _____

9. On "The Partridge Family" what is the name of the youngest son? _____

10. On "Petticoat Junction" what is the name of Betty Jo and Steve Elliott's daughter? _____

11. On "Popeye" what is the name of the baby who is Olive Oil's nephew? _____

12. On "The Flintstones" what is the name of Fred and Wilma Flintstone's daughter? _____ What is the name of Barney and Betty Rubble's son? _____

13. On "Bewitched" what are the names of Samantha and Darrin Stevens' daughter? _____ and son? _____

14. On "Blondie" what is the name of Blondie and Dagwood Bumstead's son? _____

15. On "The Dick VanDyke Show" what is the name of Rob and Laura Petrie's son?

_____

Television Tots Trivia
(correct answers)

1. Little Ricky
2. Mary, Laura and Carrie
3. Darla, Butch
4. Judy, Elroy
5. Wednesday, Pugsley
6. Steve, Charley, and Robbie Jr.
7. Eddie
8. Elizabeth
9. Chris
10. Kathy Jo
11. Swee'pea
12. Pebbles, Bamm-Bamm
13. Tabitha, Adam
14. Alexander or Baby Dumpling
15. Richie

MEMORY TESTER

Needed: Fifteen to twenty small baby-related items (e.g., pacifier, rattle, nipple, Q-tip, nail clipper, bottle washer, etc.); a tray; a cloth; pencils; paper; magazines to write on.

Prior to game: Place all of the items on a tray and cover them with a cloth.

Objective: Place the tray in the middle of the room, uncover the items, and give the players two minutes to memorize them. They are not allowed to make any notes. Cover the items again, pass out pencils and paper, and ask the players to write down as many of the baby items as they can.

The person who remembers the most items wins.

BABY TALK

Needed: A long baby phrase, such as, "Baby Betty's itty bitty bonnet fell from the pretty pink pram to a puddle, and Nanny, knitting booties, never noticed."

Objective: Players are divided into two teams, and each team sits in a circle. Start by whispering the baby phrase or message to one person on each team. That person whispers the message to the person on her right, who whispers the message to the next person, and so on. The last player in each team to hear the message announces the baby phrase out loud for everyone to hear. When they're finished, you tell all the players what the original message was.

The team that kept the message most intact wins. Each person on that team gets a prize.

PASS THE PRESENT

Needed: One present wrapped in numerous layers of blue and/or pink wrapping or tissue paper; music (preferably a lullaby).

Objective: The hostess gives the multi-wrapped present to one of the players. When the music starts, she begins passing it to her right. When the music stops, whoever has the present unwraps one layer of wrapping. The music then restarts and the present is passed again.

This continues until the last layer of wrapping is removed. That person gets to keep the present.

NAME THAT NURSERY TUNE
(see next four pages)

Needed: A music source, such as piano, organ, xylophone, kazoo, etc.; someone who can play sheet music; photocopies of "Name that Nursery Tune" game sheets; pencils; magazines to write on.

Objective: Pass out the game sheets, pencils, and magazines for players to write on. Someone plays the melodies of twelve nursery tunes, one at a time, and the players try to guess the name of each song.

The player with the most correct answers wins.

Note: Other nursery tunes can be used besides the ones listed. Check your public library for music.

Name that Nursery Tune

1. _____

2. _____

3. _____

4. _____

5. _____

6. _____

7. _____

8. _____

9. _____

10. _____

11. _____

12. _____

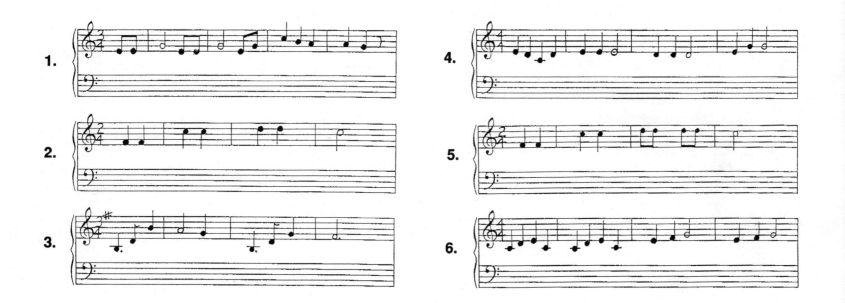

Name that Nursery Tune
(correct answers)

1. Lullaby and Goodnight/Brahms' Lullaby

2. Twinkle, Twinkle, Little Star

3. Rock-A-Bye Baby

4. Mary Had a Little Lamb

5. Baa, Baa, Black Sheep

6. Frère Jacques/Brother John

7. Hush, Little Baby/The Mocking Bird

8. Hickory, Dickory, Dock

9. London Bridge Is Falling Down

10. Sleep, Baby, Sleep

11. Here We Go Round the Mulberry Bush

12. Bye Baby Bunting

TREASURE HUNT
(see next four pages)

Needed: Treasure Hunt clues; hiding places; a small object to hide as the treasure (diaper pin, bottle cap, coin).

Prior to shower: Thoroughly clean the house and put away any personal items you don't want guests to see. Write clues on pieces of paper and hide them in sequential order, leading up to the treasure.

Objective: Players are divided into two teams and told what treasure they're looking for. Each team is given their first clue, which will tell where the next clue is hidden. Each team has different clues, but both teams' clues lead to the same treasure.

The first team to find the treasure wins. Each player on the team gets a prize.

Note: You can make up your own clues, depending on the hiding places available at the shower location. Just make sure the difficulty of the clues is balanced between the two teams.

Team One

CLUE #1
Dirty diapers, sleepers, and bibs all need to be laundered clean; this machine holds the next clue even though it's not easily seen.

CLUE #2
When baby finally arrives friends and relatives are thrilled; congratulations are mailed and this box soon gets filled.

CLUE #3
If baby is fussy and can't go to sleep, just wind up the switch and you won't hear a peep.

CLUE #4
When baby eats a meal while sitting in this chair, the food that is served will seldom stay there.

(HIDE CLUE #2)
Pin to a dry towel, throw into the washing machine.

(HIDE CLUE #3)
In the mailbox.

(HIDE CLUE #4)
Tape under a music box.

(HIDE CLUE #5)
Tape under a high chair.

Team One (continued)

CLUE #5
Mommy can't wait until baby is trained; no more diapers to change, just flush this to drain.

CLUE #6
Baby's finally napping, so take this off the hook; now Mommy can relax and read a good book.

CLUE #7
Babies are sweet just like candy; this major ingredient sure tastes dandy.

CLUE #8
Nap time or feeding time, how does Mommy know; she looks at this object and the answer will show.

(HIDE CLUE #6)
Tape on a toilet in an inconspicuous place.

(HIDE CLUE #7)
In between the pages of a book, lying next to a telephone.

(HIDE CLUE #8)
In the sugar canister in the kitchen.

(HIDDEN OBJECT)
Under or behind any type of clock—alarm, anniversary, kitchen.

Team Two

CLUE #1
Special time together Mom and baby will share; the movement back and forth shows tender loving care.

CLUE #2
These are warm and fluffy and used to make baby dry; daily baths are needed, though sometimes babies cry.

CLUE #3
Mommy needs this tool to hand feed her baby; strained peas or prunes, something good? — maybe.

CLUE #4
When raindrops start falling from clouds in the sky, just open this up and you'll keep baby dry.

(HIDE CLUE #2)
Tape under any type of rocking chair.

(HIDE CLUE #3)
In between towels in the linen closet.

(HIDE CLUE #4)
Wrap around a spoon in the silverware drawer.

(HIDE CLUE #5)
In a closed umbrella, leaning up—behind the front door.

Team Two (continued)

CLUE #5
Scared of the dark
a baby may be; but
turn this on and
light he will see.

CLUE #6
With nourishment
and care it will
grow big and
strong; just look
between the leaves
and you can't go
wrong.

CLUE #7
After baby eats,
Mommy sweeps up
the floor; to find the
next clue you must
open the door.

CLUE #8
Nap time or feeding
time, how does
Mommy know; she
looks at this object
and the answer will
show.

(HIDE CLUE #6)
Tape to a night
light or lamp shade.

(HIDE CLUE #7)
In between the
leaves of a house
plant.

(HIDE CLUE #8)
Tape to a broom or
dust pan, in the
broom closet.

(HIDDEN OBJECT)
Under or behind
any type of
clock—alarm,
anniversary,
kitchen.

STICKER DOOR PRIZE

Materials needed: One sticker.

Objective: Prior to the shower, put a sticker under one of the guests' plates. After the guests have finished their refreshments, tell them to check the bottom of their plates.

The person with the sticker under her plate wins the prize.

Note: A sticker can also be placed under a cup or saucer.

BIRTHDAY DOOR PRIZE

Materials needed: None.

Objective: Ask all of the guests what their birthday is.

Winner: Whoever has a birthday that falls closest to the baby's due date (if the shower is before the baby is born), or the actual birthday of the baby (if the shower is after the baby is born).

SPECIAL NOTE ON GAMES

If there happens to be more than one winner for a game, and only one prize, the hostess should pick a number between one and 100. The person who guesses closest to the correct number is the winner.

Chapter Six

Refreshments

A fter the games are finished, refreshments should be served to the shower guests. The key is to keep the food as simple as possible and to do the majority of the work in advance. It is up to the hostess whether a full meal is served or just dessert. This will also depend on the time of day the shower is held. Midday or early evening showers should include some kind of meal, whereas a 7:00 p.m. shower would lend itself more to just dessert.

Refreshments served buffet-style are easiest. Just remember that if guests have to eat on their laps, the food should be easy to eat. Serve finger foods or items that can be eaten with a fork—no cutting. Suggestions for main dishes include quiche, chicken/ turkey/shrimp salad, a deli tray of fresh cold cuts and cheese, etc. Accompanying the entree should be side dishes such as shrimp salad, fresh fruit (see recipes on pages 103 and 104), and fresh rolls or croissants.

If you're short of time or don't want to fuss, there's nothing wrong with buying a bucket of fried chicken, a tray of submarine sandwiches, or tacos. If it's a problem of finances, you can coordinate a pot-luck shower where each guest brings something for the meal.

For dessert, those who like to bake can try the recipes for Baby Bottle Bundt Cake (page 112), Cut-Out Sugar Cookies (page 115), or Apple Pie Squares (page 109). If you don't care to bake you can make Animal Cracker Sandwich Cookies (page 116); or it's perfectly all right to purchase a cake or ice cream pie.

Beverages should also be available for guests. Coffee, soda pop, and ice water are standbys. For something different, a punch or frozen drink is nice.

Paper plates, cups, and napkins are easiest for cleanup. However, if you don't mind the clean up, china and linen napkins can be used to save on the cost.

WILD RICE FEAST

1 cup raw wild rice (makes 8 cups cooked)

4 cups water

2 teaspoons salt

2 pounds lean ground beef (4 cups cooked, diced chicken or turkey can be substituted)

1 pound fresh mushrooms

½ cup chopped celery

½ cup chopped onions

½ cup butter

¼ cup soy sauce

2 cups sour cream

2 cans cream of mushroom soup

2 teaspoons salt

½ teaspoon pepper

½ cup slivered almonds

Cook wild rice in 4 cups water and salt for 45 minutes; drain excess water. Chop mushrooms, onions, and celery; saute in butter for 5 minutes; pour in bowl. Use same pan to brown hamburger. At the same time, heat soup (don't add additional water) and sour cream in saucepan. Drain grease from hamburger and keep in pan. Pour vegetables back into frying pan and add hot soup and sour cream. Combine with soy sauce, salt, and pepper. Add to rice. Pour everything into a casserole dish; top with almonds. Heat at 375° F for one hour. Serves 12–16.

Note: To save time, this casserole can be made the day before the shower, refrigerated, and heated prior to serving.

SIMPLE CHEESE SOUFFLE

(continued on next page)

8 slices of bread, buttered and cubed (cut off crusts)

2 cups grated cheddar cheese

7 eggs, beaten

¼ teaspoon dry mustard

¼ teaspoon salt and pepper (each)

3 cups milk

Generously grease casserole dish with butter. Layer bread cubes and cheese in dish. Combine eggs, milk, and seasonings; pour over bread and cheese. Top with extra grated cheese. Let stand for at least 8 hours in the refrigerator. Bake uncovered at 350° F for 1½ hours. *Note:* Put casserole pan in another, larger pan filled with at least one inch of water while baking. This step prevents the souffle from sticking to the dish, making cleanup easier. Serve with hot mushroom sauce.

SIMPLE CHEESE SOUFLE
(continued)

MUSHROOM SAUCE

2 cans cream of mushrooms soup

½ cup water

1 cup fresh sliced mushrooms

Combine ingredients and heat thoroughly.

Note: This recipe serves 8; adjust according to the number of guests. To save time, the souffle can be made the day before the shower, refrigerated overnight, and baked prior to serving.

SUGAR 'N' SPICE BREAD

3 cans Pillsbury Refrigerated Buttermilk Biscuits (10 per can)

½ cup granulated sugar

½ teaspoon cinnamon

½ cup butter (one stick)

¾ cup granulated sugar

¾ teaspoon cinnamon

Cut biscuits into quarters. Combine ½ cup sugar and ½ teaspoon cinnamon; roll biscuit pieces in the mixture. Place pieces in a well-greased and floured Bundt pan. Melt butter, add ¾ cup sugar and ¾ teaspoon cinnamon; pour over biscuits. Bake at 350° F for 30 minutes. Remove from oven and let stand for 10 minutes. Invert onto serving plate. Bread is best when served warm!

BABY SHRIMP SALAD

3 cups dry, small macaroni shell noodles, cooked and chilled

2 4 ¼ oz. cans tiny (baby) shrimp

5 stalks celery, diced

¼ onion, chopped

1½ cups Miracle Whip salad dressing

1 teaspoon parsley

salt and pepper to taste

Combine all ingredients, chill, and serve.

CALICO BEANS

1 pound ground beef

1 onion, chopped

2 16 oz. cans pork and beans

1 16 oz. can butter beans, drained

1 16 oz. can kidney beans (light or dark)

1 16 oz. can chili beans

½ cup Bacon Bits

¾ cup brown sugar

½ cup vinegar

1 tablespoon dry mustard

Brown ground beef with chopped onion, drain, and put in crock pot. Add other ingredients and stir until blended. Cook on low heat for at least five hours, stirring occasionally. Serve buffet style out of the crock pot.

BABY "BIB" SALAD

6 cups torn Bibb lettuce	2 tablespoons sliced green onions
½ cup grated carrots	3 hard boiled eggs, cut up
½ cup sliced fresh mushrooms	½ cup grated Parmesan cheese
½ cup sliced radishes	1 bottle Italian dressing

Combine the first six ingredients together in a large bowl; cover and chill. Just before serving, sprinkle salad with cheese, pour on dressing, and toss lightly.

FESTIVE FRUIT KABOBS

1 package 8" bamboo skewers

3 oranges, peeled and sectioned (or canned Mandarin orange segments)

1 pint fresh strawberries (or frozen)

1 pint fresh cherries (or bottled maraschino cherries)

1 pint fresh blueberries (or frozen)

1 fresh pineapple, cored, skinned, and sliced into cubes (or canned pineapple chunks)

1 cantaloupe, made into melon balls

String pieces of fruit on skewers and tie blue and/or pink bows on the ends. *Note:* Canned or frozen fruit can be substituted if fresh is not available or if hostess wants to save time. Different kinds of fruit can be used; just be sure to vary colors and sizes of fruit pieces.

WATERMELON BUGGY

1 whole watermelon

1 pint fresh strawberries

1 pint fresh blueberries

1 fresh pineapple

1 fresh cantaloupe

2 kiwifruit

paper, toothpicks, pipe cleaners, ribbon

Cut the watermelon halfway down from the top and halfway in from the side to take out a quarter section. Remove the inside of the watermelon so all that remains is the rind in the shape of a baby buggy. Cut up the watermelon fruit and the cantaloupe into chunks or melon balls. Remove core and skin of pineapple and cut fruit into chunks. Clean strawberries and blueberries. Slice kiwifruit. Store the different fruits in separate containers until just before the shower, when they are combined and placed in the watermelon buggy. To make the buggy look more realistic, cut four circles out of paper and attach them with toothpicks to resemble wheels. Join two pipe cleaners and attach to the front of the buggy as a handle. Garnish with pink and/or blue ribbons attached with toothpicks.

BABY BERRY FRUIT SALAD

2 16 oz. cans "Whole Berry" cranberry sauce

1 20 oz. can crushed pineapple

1 16 oz. package Cool Whip

2 cups miniature marshmallows

Mix all ingredients together in a bowl. Pour mixture into ungreased Bundt pan and spread evenly; cover and freeze. Remove from freezer 15 minutes before serving. Place bottom of pan in warm water for a few minutes to loosen mold from pan. Run a knife around the outside of the pan before inverting onto a serving plate. Garnish with extra cranberries.

Note: If serving appearance is not important, a 9" x 13" covered cake pan can be used to freeze as well as serve the salad.

APPLE PIE SQUARES
(continued on next page)

1 package Betty Crocker Pastry Crust Sticks (4)

12 cups Granny Smith applies (peeled and cut in wedges)

1½ cups granulated sugar

¾ cup all-purpose flour

1 tablespoon cinnamon

1 egg white

1 12" x 17" x 1" jelly roll pan or cookie sheet

Prepare two of the pastry sticks together, adding water according to the instructions on the box. Roll out in a rectangle for the bottom crust; place over pan. Cut up apples and place in a large bowl. In a small bowl thoroughly combine sugar, flour, and cinnamon. Pour sugar mixture over apples and combine; spread out coated apples evenly over bottom crust. Prepare last two pastry sticks according to instructions. Roll out in a rectangle and place over applies. Brush top with egg white. Cut a few slits in the top of the crust for cooking. Bake at 350° F for one hour. Cool completely. Drizzle with glaze in a criss-cross pattern.

APPLE PIE SQUARES
(continued)

GLAZE

2 cups powdered sugar

2 tablespoons softened butter

1 teaspoon vanilla

Work butter into powdered sugar; add vanilla. Slowly add milk until glaze is drizzable!

PITTER-PATTER PEANUT BUTTER BARS

¾ cup light corn syrup

½ cup granulated sugar

3 cups crushed corn flakes

1 18 oz. jar of your favorite peanut butter

1 16 oz. tub of ready-to-spread chocolate frosting (optional)

colored toothpicks

Heat corn syrup and sugar until dissolved; add to crushed corn flakes and peanut butter in a large bowl. Spread evenly in ungreased 9" x 13" pan; pat down with fingers. Freeze for two hours to set. Spread with chocolate frosting if desired. Cut in "baby" 1" squares and put a colored blue and/or pink toothpick in each one for easy serving.

BABY BOTTLE BUNDT CAKE

1 Bundt cake box mix with glaze

1 12 cup Bundt pan

1 baby bottle

  candy to fill bottle and garnish

Prepare Bundt cake according to the instructions on the box. Cool. Invert cake on serving plate. Glaze. Fill baby bottle with candy and put in center of cake. Garnish the cake with extra candy around the base and bottle.

Suggestions: Lemon-flavored cake decorated with lemon drops, struesel-flavored cake decorated with gummy bears.

Note: See the game entitled "Bottled Candy" on page 50. Count the pieces of candy as you put them in the baby bottle. Let the guests guess how many pieces are in the bottle. The person with the closest number gets a prize.

MESSY BARS

1 German Chocolate Cake mix

¾ cup melted butter

⅔ cup evaporated milk (not condensed)

1 14 oz. package of caramels (unwrapped)

1 6 oz. package chocolate chips

Combine cake mix, butter, and ⅓ cup milk. With a spatula, spread half of mixture evenly in greased 9" x 13" pan. Bake at 350° F for 6 minutes; remove from oven and sprinkle with chocolate chips. Melt caramels with ⅓ cup evaporated milk (works best in microwave); pour over chips. Top with remaining cake mix. Bake another 20 minutes at 350° F.

CUT-OUT SUGAR COOKIES

¾ cup butter, softened

1 cup granulated sugar

⅛ teaspoon nutmeg

1 teaspoon vanilla

1 egg

2 cups all-purpose flour

1 teaspoon baking powder

½ teaspoon salt

2 tablespoons milk

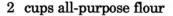

Cream butter and sugar; add nutmeg, vanilla, and egg. In separate bowl mix flour, baking powder, and salt; add to sugar mixture with milk. Form dough into ball and wrap in wax paper; chill for one hour. Roll out dough to ³⁄₁₆". Cut to desired shapes. Bake on ungreased cookie sheets at 400° F for 6–8 minutes. Decorate with colored sugar sprinkles or frosting.

Note: Cookies can be cut out in baby theme shapes (e.g., teddy bears, baby ducks, etc.). Also, if a holiday theme is being used for the shower, the appropriate shape can be made (e.g., hearts, shamrocks, pumpkins, etc.).

ANIMAL CRACKER SANDWICH COOKIES

1 large box of animal crackers   1 16 oz. tub of ready-to-spread frosting

Take one animal cracker, frost with frosting, and top with another identical animal cracker to make a sandwich cookie. Repeat until you have a full plate. Serve cookies by themselves or with ice cream.

ORANGE SHERBERT PUNCH

2 64 oz. (half gallon) cartons of orange juice

1 liter 7-Up

1 liter ginger ale

1 pint orange sherbert (softened)

4 oranges

1 Jello mold ring

The day before the shower, mix both cartons of orange juice, 7-Up, and ginger ale. Slice oranges and place slices all the way around the bottom of Jello mold ring, slightly overlapping them. Fill mold with punch mixture and freeze overnight. Refrigerate remaining mixture in covered container so it doesn't go flat. One hour before the shower, take the sherbert out of the freezer to soften. Prior to serving, add softened sherbert to punch; mix thoroughly and pour into punch bowl. Take mold out of freezer; place bottom in warm water for a few seconds until ring separates from mold. Float ring in punch (orange slices up) to keep it cold and to serve as a garnish.

Chapter Seven

Opening Gifts

G ift opening should be done toward the end of the shower so guests don't get the impression that this was the only reason they were invited.

Someone should sit next to the Mother of Honor as she opens the gifts to discreetly record who gave her which items. This list will be used for writing thank-you notes after the shower. After each gift is opened, it's nice to pass it around the room for all the guests to view. A circular seating arrangement works best.

The Mother of Honor should make certain she thanks each guest for her gift as it's opened. Once all the gifts have been opened, it's also nice for the Mother of Honor to give one large thank you to everyone for all the nice baby gifts.

MOTHERLY ADVICE

A final, shared gift for the Mother of Honor from all of the guests might be a list of motherly advice (see next page). Pass around a sheet of paper on which each guest can write down one piece of advice for the new mother. Some examples might be, "You can never rock a baby too much," or "Pack your diaper bag the night before an outing." This is a unique gift that the Mother of Honor will appreciate for years to come.

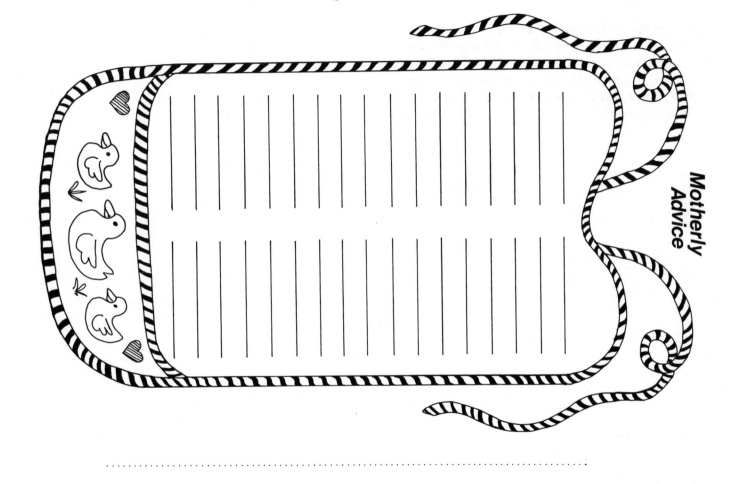

Motherly
Advice

GIFT CARD COLLAGE

Another memento from the baby shower for the Mother of Honor would be a collage made from the gift cards. Simply take a piece of paper and tape all of the gift cards to it. The collage can later be put in the baby's scrap book.

Chapter Eight

Ending the Shower

As guests leave, both you and the Mother of Honor should thank them for coming and escort them to the door. When all the guests have gone, help the Mother of Honor pack up all of the gifts and get them to her car.

Written thank-you notes should be mailed out by the Mother of Honor within one week of the shower. After the baby is born, it's nice if the new mother calls or sends birth announcements to all of the shower guests to let them know.